# Classic Country

Production Manager: Daniel Rosenbaum
Art Direction: Kerstin Fairbend
Administration: Monica Corton
Director of Music: Mark Phillips

ISBN: 0-89524-595-7

# CONTENTS

4    Ace In The Hole
As recorded by GEORGE STRAIT

8    All The Fun
As recorded by PAUL OVERSTREET

12    Annie's Song
As recorded by JOHN DENVER

16    Any Way The Wind Blows
As recorded by SOUTHERN PACIFIC

20    The Battle Hymn Of Love
As recorded by KATHY MATTEA and TIM O'BRIEN

24    Bayou Boys
As recorded by EDDY RAVEN

27    Deeper Than The Holler
As recorded by RANDY TRAVIS

30    The Dance
As recorded by GARTH BROOKS

34    Dear Me
As recorded by LORRIE MORGAN

37    Diggin' Up Bones
As recorded by RANDY TRAVIS

40    Drive South
As recorded by JOHN HIATT

45    The Flower That Shattered The Stone
As recorded by JOHN DENVER

49    Fly On The Wall
As recorded by EXILE

52    Fly Away
As recorded by JOHN DENVER

56    Folsom Prison Blues
As recorded by JOHNNY CASH

CHERRY LANE MUSIC: THE PRINT COMPANY

**EXECUTIVE:** Michael Lefferts, President; Kathleen A. Maloney, Director of Advertising and Promotion; Rock Stamberg, Assistant Director of Advertising and Promotion; Len Handler, Creative Services Manager; Monica C
Contracts Administrator; Karen Carey, Division Secretary; Karen DeCrenza, Executive Secretary.
**MUSIC:** Mark Phillips, Director of Music; Jon Chappell, Associate Director of Music; Gordon Hallberg, Computer Music Engraver; Steve Gorenberg, Music Editor; Kerry O'Brien, Music Editor; Cathy Cassinos-Carr, Copy
**ART:** Kerstin A. Fairbend, Art Director; Michele Lyons, Assistant Art Director; Rosemary Cappa, Art Assistant.
**PRODUCTION:** Daniel Rosenbaum, Production Manager; James Piacentino, Production Coordinator.

58    Forever & Ever, Amen
As recorded by RANDY TRAVIS

62    Full Moon Full Of Love
As recorded by K.D. LANG AND
THE RECLINES

65    Honky Tonk Moon
As recorded by RANDY TRAVIS

68    Goin' Gone
As recorded by KATHY MATTEA

72    The Highwayman
As recorded by THE HIGHWAYMEN

75    Houston Solution
As recorded by RONNIE MILSAP

78    I Fell In Love
As recorded by CARLENE CARTER

82    I Won't Take Less Than Your Love
As recorded by TANYA TUCKER WITH
PAUL DAVIS and PAUL OVERSTREET

88    Lady
As recorded by KENNY ROGERS

92    Love Chooses You
As recorded by KATHY MATTEA

97    On The Other Hand
As recorded by RANDY TRAVIS

100    My Arms Stay Open All Night
As recorded by TANYA TUCKER

104    Love Or Something Like It
As recorded by KENNY ROGERS

109    Out Of Your Shoes
As recorded by LORRIE MORGAN

112    The Night's Too Long
As recorded by PATTY LOVELESS

117    Reckless Heart
As recorded by SOUTHERN PACIFIC

120    Postcard From Paris
As recorded by JOHN DENVER

124    Seein' My Father In Me
As recorded by PAUL OVERSTREET

128    She Came From Fort Worth
As recorded by KATHY MATTEA

133    Sowin' Love
As recorded by PAUL OVERSTREET

138    Take Me Home, Country Roads
As recorded by JOHN DENVER

141    Still Within The Sound Of My Voice
As recorded by GLEN CAMPBELL

146    This Little Town
As recorded by DAVE MALLETT

151    When I Could Come Home To You
As recorded by STEVE WARINER

154    Unanswered Prayers
As recorded by GARTH BROOKS

159    When You Say Nothing At All
As recorded by KEITH WHITLEY

162    Where Did I Go Wrong
As recorded by STEVE WARINER

164    Wichita Lineman
As recorded by GLEN CAMPBELL

166    Wrong
As recorded by WAYLON JENNINGS

# ACE IN THE HOLE

## As recorded by GEORGE STRAIT

Words and Music by
Dennis Adkins

ble,   a game___ we all play,___   but you need to save   some - thing for a rain - y day.___

You've got to learn___ to play your cards___ right

if you ex - pect to

win ___ in life. ___ Don't

put it all ___ on the line ___ for just ___ one

roll. You've got to have ___ an ace ___ in the hole. ___

2. If you're
3. You've

No mat-ter what_you do, no mat-ter where_ you go, you've got to have_ an ace _____ in the hole.__

*Additional Lyrics*

2. If you're headed down a one-way street
   And you're not sure it's the way you want to go,
   And money or love, or all the above,
   Have a little more than what you show.
   When life deals out a surprise,
   Have a few surprises of your own.
   No matter what you do,
   No matter where you go,
   You've got to have an ace in the hole.

3. *Repeat 1st Verse*

# ALL THE FUN

## As recorded by PAUL OVERSTREET

Words and Music by
Paul Overstreet and Taylor Dunn

can't un-der-stand why a mar-ried man_ is in a hur - ry to ev - er go_ home.

Chorus

I just tell them that_ all the fun that I'm ev - er gon - na need I got_ wait - in' at home_ for me._ Yeah, she likes to dance,_ and she loves_ _ ro - mance, and she throws a great par - ty. There's nev - er an - y dull min - utes a - round here,_ some - thin' al - ways a - go - in' on._

All the fun_ that a man_ could want, I got wait - in' for me at_ home.

_

2. Hey, I

We got two lit - tle kids_ call - in' me Dad - dy,

run - nin' all o - ver the house._ When they fi - n'lly go to sleep, their ma - ma and me

cud - dle and we snug - gle and we par - ty on the couch._

Yeah, I got

*Additional Lyrics*

2. Hey, I used to be a fool, and a sucker for a high time,
Any time night or day.
I had a round-the-clock smile, just call me and I would be
Readily on my way.
But to tell you the truth, I was lonesome and blue,
Prayin' for a little light in my life.
Then a miracle came, and everything changed,
And I made that little woman my wife.
Let me tell you that ... *(To Chorus)*

# ANNIE'S SONG

## As recorded by JOHN DENVER

Words and Music by
John Denver

# ANY WAY THE WIND BLOWS

## As recorded by SOUTHERN PACIFIC

Words and Music by
John McFee and Andre Pessis

where the wind blows, ____

*Repeat and fade*

an - y - where the wind blows, ____

*Additional Lyrics*

2. Burnin' both ends of the candle,
   Can't worry about the things that we don't know.
   Goin' just as fast as we can go,
   Any way the wind blows.
   Doesn't matter if we lead or follow,
   No tellin' where we'll be tomorrow.
   Goin' somewhere, goin' full throttle,
   Any way the wind blows.

   *2nd Chorus:*
   And we don't know what lies in store,
   But still we walk through that open door.
   We just go any way the wind blows.

3. Who can say what might have been,
   We gotta play out the hand we're given.
   Take a ride to the place we're driven,
   Any way the wind blows.

   *3rd Chorus:*
   And we can't see around the bend,
   We never know where the road might end.
   We just go any way the wind blows, *etc.*

# THE BATTLE HYMN OF LOVE

### As recorded by KATHY MATTEA and TIM O'BRIEN

Words and Music by
Paul Overstreet and Don Schlitz

I'll for-sake my __ rest __ for your hap-pi-ness; __ till my death I will stand by __ you. __

Chorus

With God as my wit-ness __ this vow I will __ make, __ to have and to hold __ you, no oth-er to take. __

will not run.___ Till my death I ___ will stand by ___

you. ___

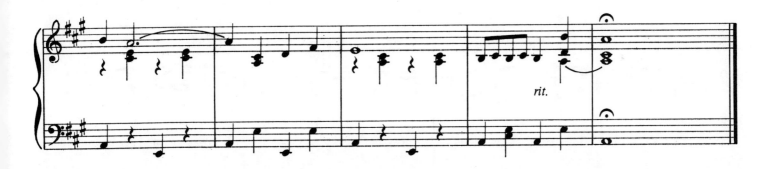

*rit.*

*Additional Lyrics*

2. There are wars and there are rumors,
The wars yet to come.
Temptations we'll have to walk through.
Though others may tremble
I will not run.
Till my death I will stand by you.

*2nd Chorus*: I will put on the armor of faithfulness
To fight for a heart that is true.
Till the battle is won
I will not rest.
Till my death I will stand by you.

# BAYOU BOYS

As recorded by EDDY RAVEN

Words and Music by
Frank J. Myers, Eddy Raven
and Troy Seals

*Additional Lyrics*

2. Me and my friend Albo, he's the one who had the car.
   We made all the dances, we made all the bars.
   Told each other secrets and we wore each other's clothes.
   One night I stole his woman and I wonder if he knows. *(To Chorus)*

3. Sweet Marie was dangerous with those dark, seductive eyes.
   She had me sayin', "Maybe, babe" before I realized.
   She loved me so deeply and I tried to hold on,
   But changin' don't come easy when you've been this way so long. *(To Chorus)*

# DEEPER THAN THE HOLLER

## As recorded by RANDY TRAVIS

Words and Music by
Paul Overstreet and Don Schlitz

# THE DANCE

## As recorded by GARTH BROOKS

Words and Music by
Tony Arata

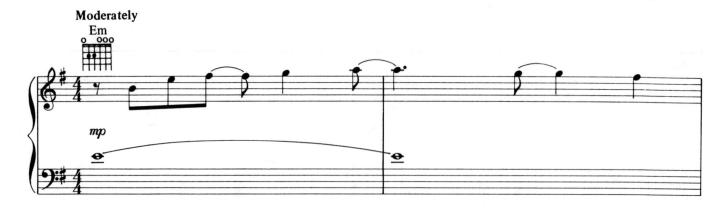

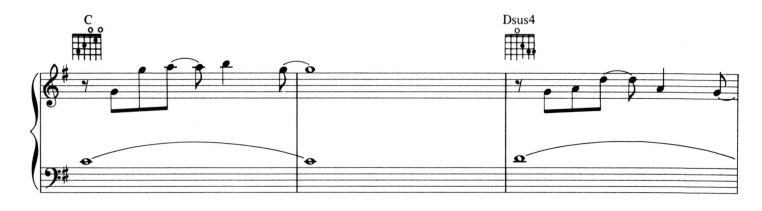

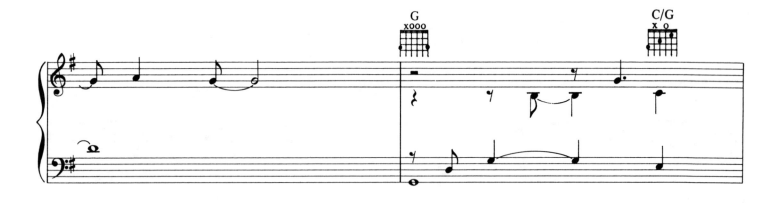

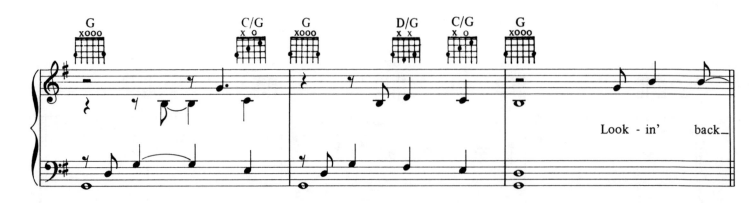

Look - in' back_

I'm glad I did-n't know the way it all would end, the way it all would go. Our lives {1.2. are}{3. it's} bet-ter left to chance. I could have missed the pain, but I'd-a had to miss the

# DEAR ME

## As recorded by LORRIE MORGAN

Words and Music by
Scott Mateer and Carson Whitsett

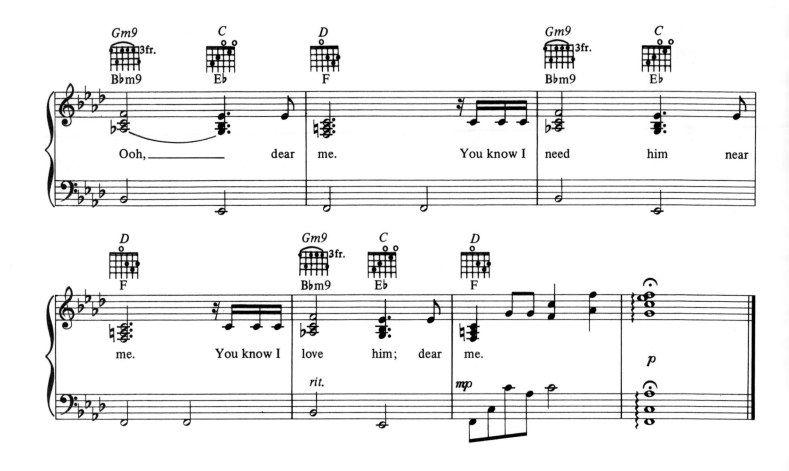

2. Dear me
   Do you really mind?
   You're the only friend
   Who will take the time
   To hear me.
   Oh, and all the plans we've made,
   If he'll take me back,
   I'll do anything to make him stay.

*2nd Chorus:*
Dear me
We'll start all over again,
Oh, and near me
I hope he'll stay till the end.
If he could see me now
Sittin' here all alone,
If he could read these words
Would he run back home?
Dear me.

# DIGGIN' UP BONES

## As recorded by RANDY TRAVIS

Words and Music by
Paul Overstreet, Al Gore,
and Nat Stuckey

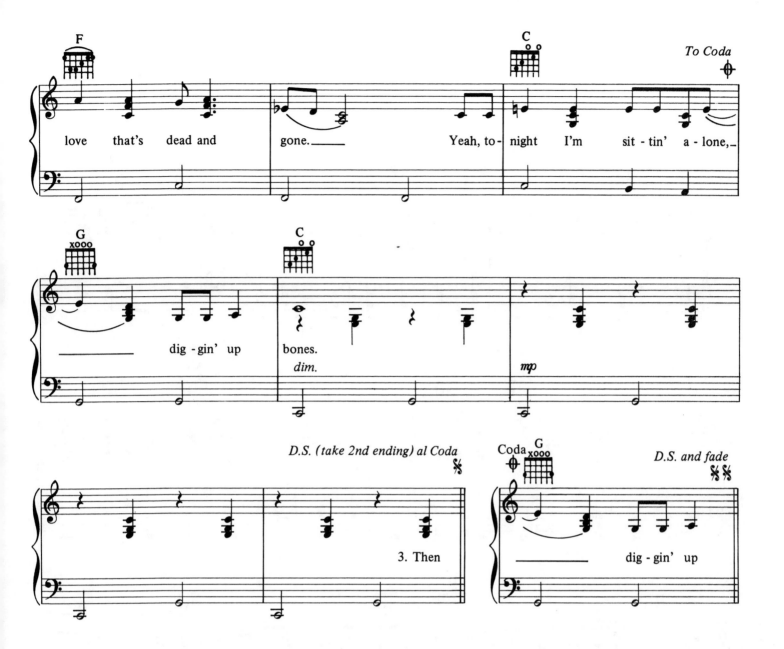

*Additional Lyrics*

2. Then I went through the jewelry,
   And I found our wedding rings.
   I put mine on my finger,
   And I gave yours a fling
   Across this lonely bedroom
   Of our recent broken home.
   Yeah, tonight I'm sittin' alone,
   Diggin' up bones. *(To Chorus)*

3. Then I went through the closet,
   And I found some things in there,
   Like that pretty negligee
   That I bought you to wear.
   And I recalled how good you looked
   Each time you put it on.
   Yeah, tonight I'm sittin' alone,
   Diggin' up bones. *(To Chorus)*

# DRIVE SOUTH

## As recorded by JOHN HIATT

Words and Music by
John Hiatt

I did-n't say__ we would-n't hurt an-y-more,__that's how you learn,___ you just get
I'm not talk-in' 'bout re-treat-in', lit-tle girl,gon-na take our stand___ in this Chev-y

burned.__ But we don't have to feel like dirt an-y-more;_though love's not
van.___ Win-dows o-pen on the rest of the world,_ hold-in'

Come on, ba - by, drive ____ south ____ with the one you ____

love.                        (Spoken:) I heard your mama callin',

I think she was just stallin'. Don't know who she was talkin' to.   Ba - by, me and you.

We could go down with a smile ____ on.   Don't both - er to pack your ny - lons,

*Pianists: omit high B.

43

*Repeat and fade*

# THE FLOWER THAT SHATTERED THE STONE

## As recorded by JOHN DENVER

Words by Joe Henry
Music by John Jarvis

The

earth is our moth - er, just turn - ing a - round, with her
Spar - rows find free - dom be - hold - ing the_ sun. In the

trees in the for - est and roots un - der_ ground. _____ Our
in - fi - nite beau - ty we're all joined in _ one. _____ I

fa - ther_ a - bove us whose sigh is the_ wind,
reach out _ be - fore me and look to the_ sky. Did I

paint us a rain - bow _ with - out an - y end.}
hear some - one whis - per? _ Did some - thing pass by?}

As the riv - er _ runs free - ly, the moun - tain does_

Like a bright star in heav- en that lights our way home, like the flow- er___ that shat-tered the stone.___

*rit.*

# FLY ON THE WALL

## As recorded by EXILE

Music by Bruce Hornsby
Words by Bernie Taupin

tooth brush tucked up your sleeve,— mak-ing love through the night— be-neath a bare light,— just a

shake - down in sec-ond-hand sheets? And a

Chorus

dia-mond can't buy the lies— that you hide—when you tell— me a friend— took a fall. — And I'd

pay an-y price— just for one night— if I— were a fly— on the wall. — Just to

look down and see your sweet poi - son,— oh, to hear— your— love call.— Just a

*Additional Lyrics*

2. There's the silver Mercedes that I never rode in.
   Where's your pool hall Don Juan with his ruby red stick pin?
   He's naked as daybreak and hungry for you
   As your footsteps approach him in room twenty-two.
   Do you really believe this one's for keeps?
   Does his silver tongue send you insane?
   Will he promise you life as his sweetheart and wife
   When he barely remembers your name? *(To Chorus)*

# FLY AWAY

As recorded by JOHN DENVER

Words and Music by
John Denver

Fly a-way,____ Fly a-way.____

*To Coda* ⊕

Life in the cit - y can make you cra - zy For sounds of the sand____ and the sea.____
look-ing for lov - ers and chil-dren play - ing, She's look-ing for signs____ of the spring.____

____ Life in a high - rise can make you hun - gry For
____ She lis-tens for laugh - ter and sounds of danc - ing, She

# FOLSOM PRISON BLUES

## As recorded by JOHNNY CASH

Words and Music by
John R. Cash

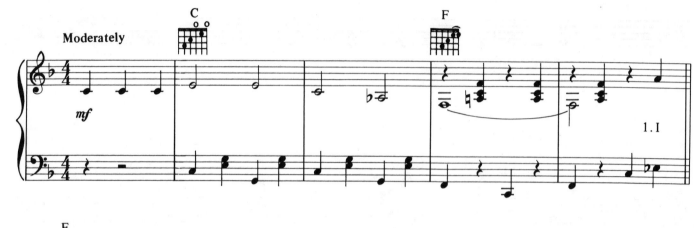

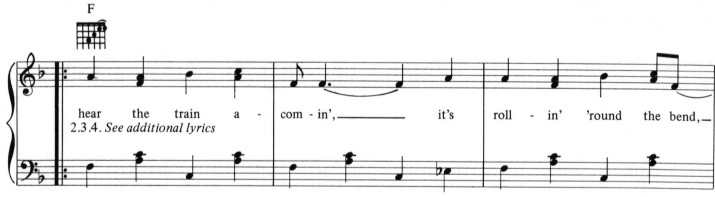

hear the train a - com - in', _____ it's roll - in' 'round the bend, _____

2.3.4. *See additional lyrics*

_____ and I ain't seen the sun - shine since I don't_ know

when. I'm stuck in Fol - som pris - on and time keeps

*Additional Lyrics*

2. When I was just a baby, my mama told me, son,
   Always be a good boy, don't ever play with guns.
   But I shot a man in Reno just to watch him die.
   When I hear that whistle blowin', I hang my head and cry.

3. I bet there's rich folks eatin' from a fancy dining car.
   They're prob'ly drinkin' coffee and smokin' big cigars.
   Well, I know I had it comin'. I know I can't be free,
   But those people keep a-movin' and that's what tortures me.

4. Well, if they freed me from this prison,
   If that railroad train was mine,
   I bet I'd move it on a little farther down the line,
   Far from Folsom prison, that's where I want to stay.
   And I'd let that lonesome whistle blow my blues away.

# FOREVER AND EVER, AMEN

As recorded by RANDY TRAVIS

Words and Music by
Paul Overstreet and Don Schlitz

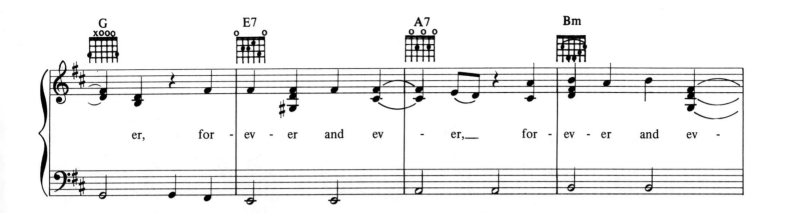

er, for - ev - er and ev - er,__ for - ev - er and ev -

er,__ for - ev - er and ev - er,__ a - men.

Tacet

freely

mp

## Additional Lyrics

2. You're not just time that I'm killing.
   I'm no longer one of those guys.
   As sure as I live, this love that I give
   Is gonna be yours until the day that I die. *(To Chorus)*

3. They say time takes its toll on a body,
   Makes a young girl's brown hair turn gray.
   Well honey, I don't care. I ain't in love with your hair.
   And if it all fell out I'd love you anyway.

4. Well, they say time can play tricks on a memory,
   Make people forget things they knew.
   Well, it's easy to see it's happening to me.
   I've already forgotten every woman but you. *(To Chorus)*

# FULL MOON FULL OF LOVE

As recorded by K.D. LANG AND THE RECLINES

Words and Music by
Leroy Preston and Jeannie Smith

Coy - o - te, oh, coy - o - te,
Ba - by, oh, sweet ba - by,

can you tell me why___
can you ex - plain this,___
ev - 'ry time___ the big___ moon shines___ you
ev - 'ry time___ the big___ moon shines___ I

sit right  down and  cry. _____
fi - n'lly  get  a  kiss. _____  Said it's not  be - cause _ I'm  sad that I __
Said it's just  the moon -  beams that make __

__ sing all __ night  long.  I'm  look - in' for __ some - one  to love __  and
__ you do __ these  things.  I  think that  I'll __  just  sit  right here __  and

this is  my love  song.  Ooh, _____  oh,  I  go
like that  coy - ote  sing.

cra -  zy  when that  moon _____  shines a - bove. __

# HONKY TONK MOON

## As recorded by RANDY TRAVIS

Words and Music by
Dennis O'Rourke

66

# GOIN' GONE

## As recorded by KATHY MATTEA

Words and Music by
Fred Koller, Pat Alger
and Bill Dale

ver,_____
ing,_____

that I would look for love_____ no more.__
I swear it's mine and com - ing in.__

Chorus

Deep in the wa - ters_____ of love__

I am fall - ing,_____ sink - ing_____ like a

stone._____ Deep in my heart I can

D.S. and fade on Chorus

71

# THE HIGHWAYMAN

## As recorded by THE HIGHWAYMEN

Words and Music by
Jimmy Webb

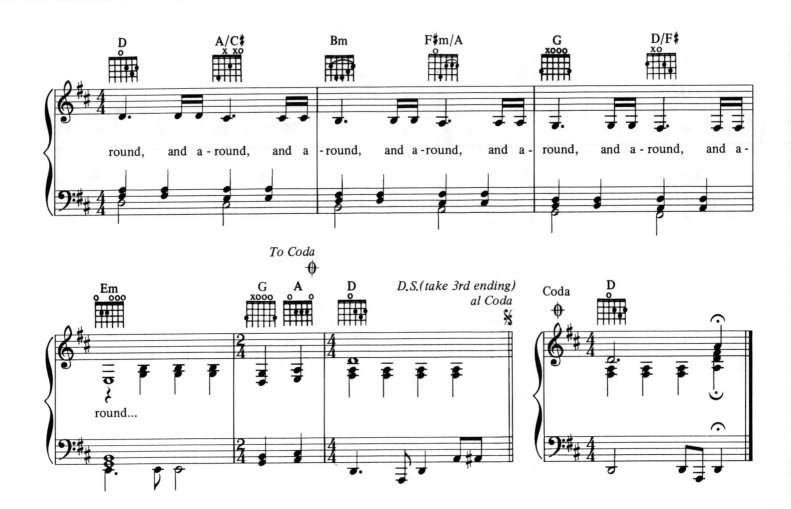

*Additional Lyrics*

2. I was a sailor,
   And I was born upon the tide,
   And with the sea I did abide.
   I sailed a schooner 'round the Horn to Mexico;
   I went aloft to furl the mainsail in a blow.
   And when the yards broke off, they say that I got killed.
   But I am living still...

3. I was a dam builder
   Across the river deep and wide,
   Where steel and water did collide,
   A place called Boulder on the wild Colorado.
   I slipped and fell into the wet concrete below.
   They buried me in that great tomb that knows no sound,
   But I am still around;
   I'll always be around, and around, and around,
   And around, and around, and around, and around...

4. I'll fly a starship
   Across the universe divide.
   And when I reach the other side,
   I'll find a place to rest my spirit if I can.
   Perhaps I may become a highwayman again,
   Or I may simply be a single drop of rain.
   But I will remain.
   And I'll be back again, and again, and again,
   And again, and again, and again , and again...

# HOUSTON SOLUTION

As recorded by RONNIE MILSAP

Words and Music by
Paul Overstreet and Don Schlitz

Easy Country Waltz

*(lyrics)*

I've got some

friends down in Hous-ton ___ who know me ___ quite well. They'll
dad-dy once told me, ___ you you can't run ___ a-way. Your

be more ___ than hap-py ___ to put me up for ___ a spell.
trou-bles ___ will fol-low ___ and up find you ___ some-day.

I can hang out ___ or hide out, ___ which-ev-er I
There's no use ___ to ar-gue, ___ 'cause he's prob-'bly

choose,       and they won't ask _____ me ques- tions _____ 'bout why I've got _____ the
right.       But I've run out _____ of op- tions _____ and I'm leav - in' _____ to -

blues. _____
night. _____      I've got a Hous- ton so- lu - tion _____ in mind. _____

All it takes _____ is a call on _____ the tel - e - phone

line. _____     And I can leave all     the prob- lems _____ of

# I FELL IN LOVE

## As recorded by CARLENE CARTER

Words and Music by
Carlene Carter, Howie Epstein,
Perry Lamek and Benmont Tench

be like this; you got___ the kind of charm that I can't re - sist.___ I

D    G
fig - ure, what's the harm in a lit - tle bit - ty kiss or two?___ But I fell in

Chorus
C    G
love.___ (What - cha wan - na do that for?) I fell in

C    G
love.___ (What - cha wan - na do that for?) I fell in

C    D
love.

Took___ me by sur - prise,___ put me
Did - n't see you com - ing___

on the floor, right be - tween the eyes with a two - by - four. Just
in - to view, I was o - ver - whelmed and o - ver - due. I

ain't a lit - tle taste, and
gon - na sweat it, I fell in love.

G

1.

2.

Well, I fell in

C                                    G

love. (What - cha wan - na do that for?) I fell in

C                                    G

love. (What - cha wan - na do that for?) I fell in

love.____

Caught____ me on the blind - side____
Try'n'____ to vi - su'l - ize____ what's____

un - a - ware; may be a fool,____ but____ I don't care. I
wrong with me; got me hyp - no - tized,____ I____ can - not see.

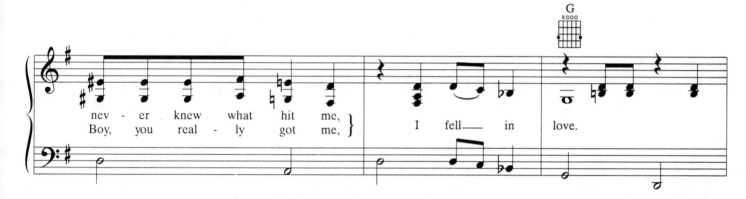

nev - er knew what hit me, } I fell____ in love.
Boy, you real - ly got me,

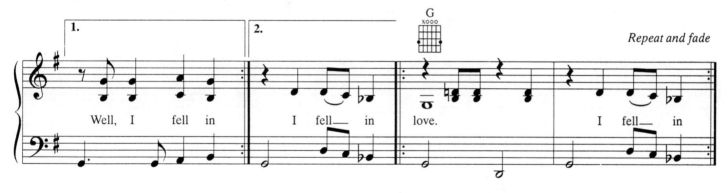

**1.**
Well, I fell in

**2.**
I fell____ in love.

*Repeat and fade*

I fell____ in

*Additional Lyrics*

2. I was doing fine out on my own,
   Never sitting home by the telephone.
   I couldn't complain that I didn't have much to do.
   I was a two-fisted woman looking for a fight;
   Had a boy on my left, a boy on the right.
   But you burn me up like a chicken in a barbecue. *(To Chorus)*

# I WON'T TAKE LESS THAN YOUR LOVE

## As recorded by TANYA TUCKER with PAUL DAVIS and PAUL OVERSTREET

Words and Music by
Paul Overstreet and Don Schlitz

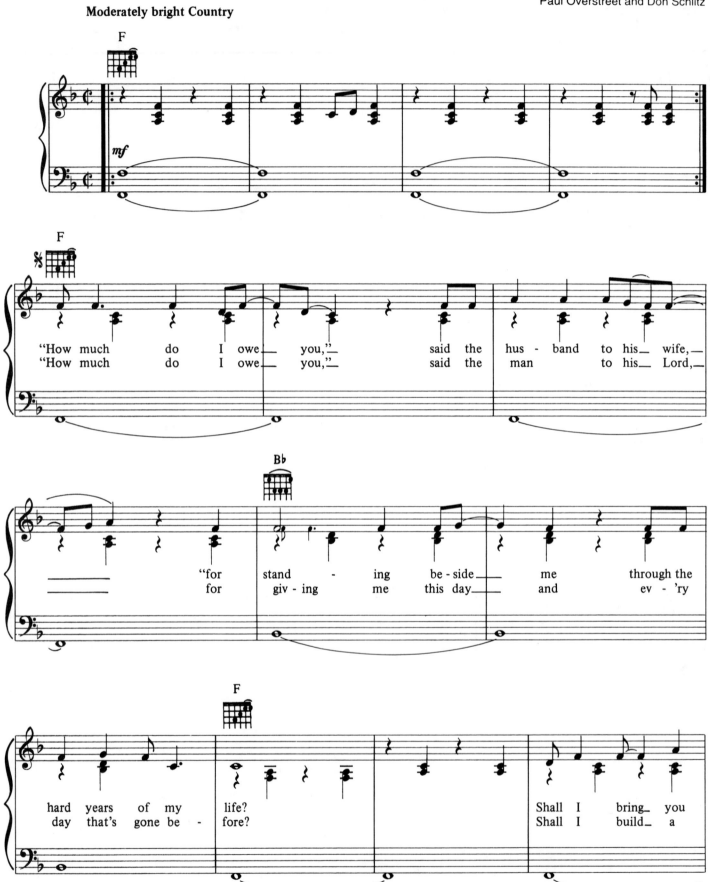

"How much do I owe you," said the hus - band to his wife, —
"How much do I owe you," said the man to his Lord, —

"for stand - ing be - side me through the
for giv - ing me this day and ev - 'ry

hard years of my life?
day that's gone be - fore?

Shall I bring you
Shall I build a

dia - monds?          Shall I    buy___      you    furs?_____
tem - ple?    Shall I    make a    sac - ri - fice?_____

Say_____    the word_____    and    it's    yours."___
Tell    me Lord,_    and I ___    will    pay    the    price."___

And his wife said,⎰ "I    won't    take    less    than your    love,    sweet
And the Lord said,⎰

love.___    No, I    won't    take    less    than your    love.___

com - forts of the world _____ could nev - er be e - nough, _____ and I

won't _ take less than your love."_____

*D.S. al Coda*

won't take less ... I won't take less than your

love,  sweet  love.  No, I  won't  take  less  than your

love.      All  the  treas - ures of the world    could

nev - er  be e - nough.  And I  won't take  less  than your

love.    No, I  won't take  less  than your

love"

# LADY

## As recorded by KENNY ROGERS

Words and Music by
Lionel Richie

* Recorded 1/2 step higher, in E♭ minor

To Coda

hold you in my arms for - ev - er more.___ You have
hear you whis-per soft-ly ___ in my ear. In my

gone ___ and made me such a fool, ___ I'm ___ so lost in your

love. And oh, ___ we be - long to - geth - er,

D.S. al Coda

Won't you be - lieve ___ in my song? ___

89

# LOVE CHOOSES YOU

## As recorded by KATHY MATTEA

Words and Music by
Laurie Lewis

down        to your__ shoes._____        It knows heart-ache        and

trial _____        but ac-cepts no_____ de-ni-al.__

You can't        choose who you        love,__        love choos-es you.__

1.                                2. D/E                A
E

2. In the                                Tell__ me now if I'm__ wrong.__

Chorus

Are__ you feel - in' the same?__

Are__ your feet____ on__ the ground?____

Are__ you call - ing____ my__ name?__

Do__ you lie a - wake__ nights?__

Please__ say____ you do.__

'Cause\_ you can't choose\_
who you\_ love, love chooses you.\_

*straight ♪'s* - - - - - - - - - - - -

*To Coda*

*D.S. (with repeat)*
*al Coda*

3. Love

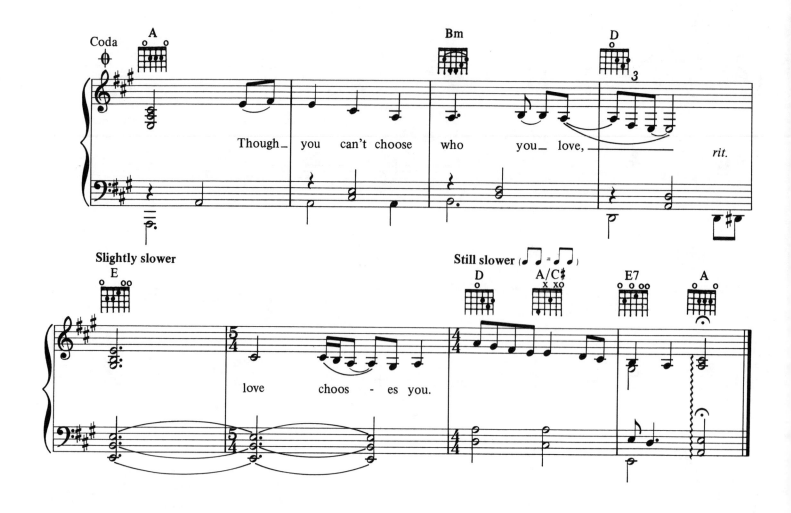

*Additional Lyrics*

2. In the wink of an eye love looses an arrow.
   We control it no more than the flight of the sparrow,
   The swell of the tide or the light of the moon.
   You can't choose who you love, love chooses you. *(To Chorus)*

3. Love cuts like a torch to a heart behind steel,
   And though you may hide it, love knows how you feel.
   And though you may trespass on the laws of the land,
   Your heart has to follow when love takes your hand.

4. And it seems we're two people within the same circle;
   It's drawn tighter and tighter till you're all that I see.
   I'm full and I'm empty and you're pouring through me
   Like a warm rain fallin' through the leaves on a tree. *(To Chorus)*

# ON THE OTHER HAND

## As recorded by RANDY TRAVIS

Words and Music by
Paul Overstreet and Don Schlitz

hand there's no rea-son why it's wrong.
But on the

*cresc.*

**Chorus**

oth-er hand
there's a gold-en band
to re-

*mf*

mind me of some-one who would not un-der-stand.
On

one hand I could stay
and be your lov-ing man,
but the

*Additional Lyrics*

2. In your arms I feel the passion I thought had died;
When I looked into your eyes, I found myself.
And when I first kissed your lips, I felt so alive.
I've got to hand it to you girl, you're something else. *(To Chorus)*

# MY ARMS STAY OPEN ALL NIGHT

## As recorded by TANYA TUCKER

Words and Music by
Paul Overstreet and Don Schlitz

ments_____ and I want - ed you_____ to know,_____

when all the laugh - ter's end - ed _____ there's still some - where you can_ go.__

Chorus
My arms stay o - pen all__ night,

from sun - down till the morn - ing light.__ Hop - ing you can find__

_ where_ you_ be - long,_____ I leave the lights_ on._

101

My heart is nev-er closed. You're the on - ly

love it knows. The one dream I have is to hold you tight.

My arms stay o-pen all night.

*To Coda*

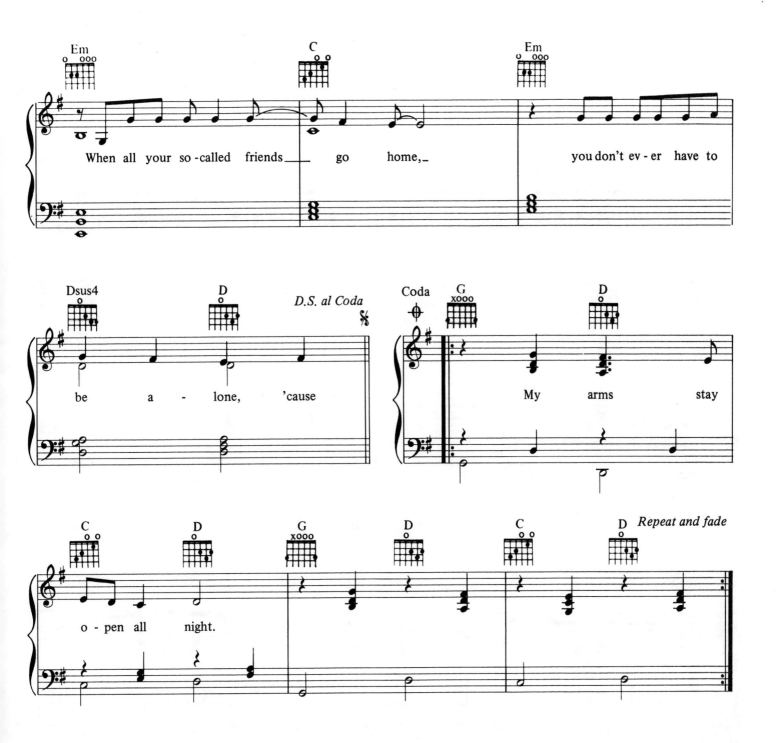

When all your so-called friends_ go home,_ you don't ev-er have to be a - lone, 'cause

*D.S. al Coda*

My arms stay o - pen all night.

*Repeat and fade*

**Additional Lyrics**

2. Please don't think I'm crazy,
   I haven't lost my mind,
   But when it comes to loving you
   I can always find the time.
   So if it's after midnight
   Or just before the break of day,
   Any time you need me
   It'll never be too late. *(To Chorus)*

# LOVE OR SOMETHING LIKE IT

As recorded by KENNY ROGERS

Words and Music by
Kenny Rogers and Steve Glassmeyer

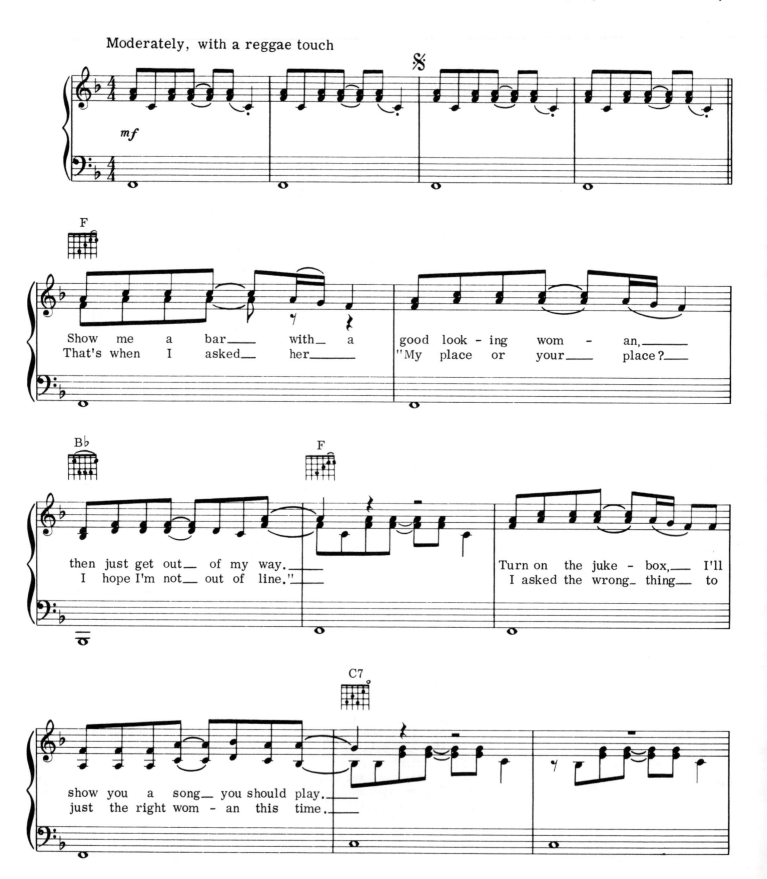

Soon - er or lat - er,_____ a | few shots of bour - bon,_____
She knew a ho - tel,_____ she | e - ven had a name we could

I'll think of some-thing to say.___ | Wo,___ I can | take her or leave_ her___
sign._____ | Wo,___ the | cheap-er the grapes_ are _ the

*To Coda* ⊕

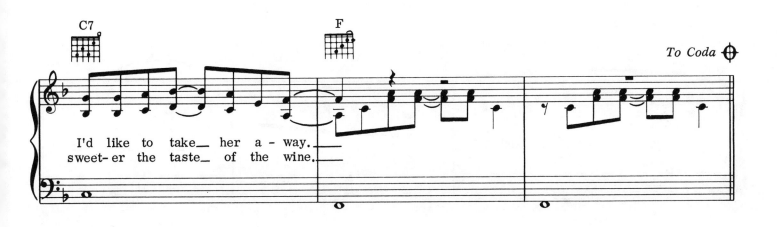

I'd like to take_ her a - way.___ |
sweet- er the taste_ of the wine.___ |

Li-quor and mu - sic,_ A | good com-bi - na - tion_ | if you've got love_ on the brain._

I nev - er knew__ two__ wom - en who act - ed the same:__

Some want a drink__ first__ and

some want to just__ sit and talk.__ Wo,_____ it's

two in the morn - ing__ I'm run-ning and she wants to walk.

# OUT OF YOUR SHOES

As recorded by LORRIE MORGAN

Words and Music by
Sharon Marie Spivey, Jill Wood,
Sharon Spivey James and Patti Ryan

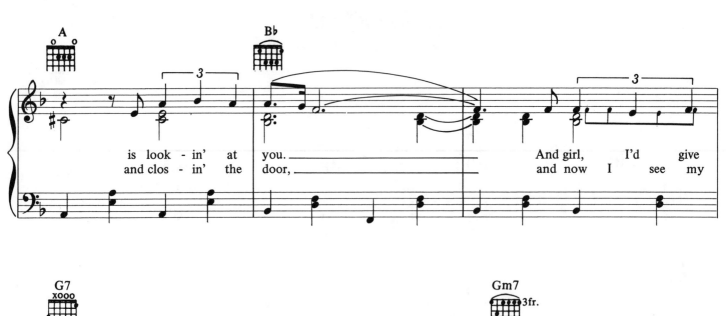

is look - in' at you. ___ And girl, I'd give
and clos - in' the door, ___ and now I see my

an - y - thing ___ to be in your ___ shoes. ___
fa - v'rite ___ dress ___ fall to the ___ floor. ___

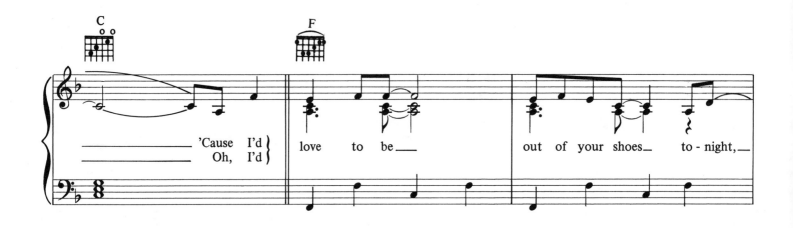

___ 'Cause I'd } love to be ___ out of your shoes ___ to - night, ___
___ Oh, I'd }

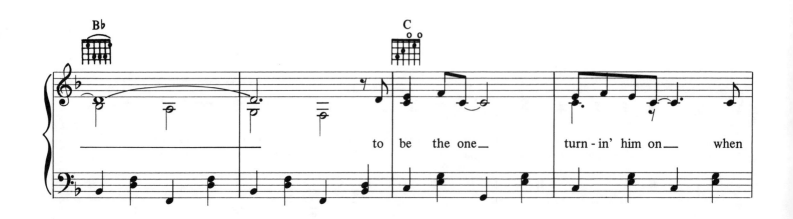

___ to be the one ___ turn - in' him on ___ when

# THE NIGHT'S TOO LONG

As recorded by PATTY LOVELESS

Words and Music by
Lucinda Williams

town boys,— they don't move fast e - nough.— I'm gon-na

find me one— who wears a leath-er jack - et and likes his— liv-in' rough."—

So she saved— her tips and o-ver-time— and

bought an old rust - y car.— She sold most— ev-'ry-thing—

— she had— to make a brand-new start. She said, "I

don't want it to end.

*rit.*

## Additional Lyrics

2. Well, she works in an office now,
And she guesses the pay's alright.
She can buy a few new things to wear
And still go out at night.
And as soon as she get home from work,
She wants to be out with a crowd
Where she can dance and toss her head back
And laugh out loud.

Well, the music's playin' fast
And they just met.
He presses up against her,
And his shirt's all soaked with sweat.
And with her back against the bar,
She can listen to the band.
And she's holdin' a Corona,
And it's cold against her hand. *(To Chorus)*

# RECKLESS HEART

As recorded by SOUTHERN PACIFIC

Words and Music by
Andre Pessis and John McFee

Walk-in' through a morn-in' af-ter,___ a dead - end
Winds___ blow-in' off the riv - er,___ head-in' out to

love___ af-fair,___ a jour-ney down a road of pas-sion
who___ knows where.___ Leav-ing just a chill be-hind it,

that led no - where.___

then it dis - ap - pears.___

May - be it's the

Guess we got a

chang - in' weath - er,___

feels a lit - tle

cold___ to - day.___

lot in com - mon,___

here to - day and

then___ we're gone.___

May - be it's just

You can feel it

get - tin' hard - er___

pass - in' by you,___

to walk a -

but you can't hold

way.___

on.___

Reck - less

heart,___

dreams a - ban -

doned.___

Gone too

soon,___

the love___ you

start (the love you start). Fall - ing fast,_____ nev - er land -

ing._____ When will true_____ love tame this reck - less heart?_

D.S. and fade

Dreams a - ban -

# POSTCARD FROM PARIS

## As recorded by JOHN DENVER

Words and Music by
Jimmy Webb

I wish you were here___ (when the shad-ows fall and all the rush-ing traf-fic stills).___ I
I wish you were here___ (on the Champs-El- y - sées lov - ers walk-ing hand in hand).___ I

wish you were here (and the bells are ring - ing on___ the Sev - en___ Hills)..___ I
wish you were here (they take one look at me___ and seem___ to un - der - stand).. This

make my way___ to a small ca - fé;___ I won - der what_ you did to - day ...___
cit - y of light is a love - ly sight;___ the first bright star_ I see to - night ...___

Wish you were here.___

# SEEIN' MY FATHER IN ME

As recorded by PAUL OVERSTREET

Words and Music by
Paul Overstreet and Taylor Dunn

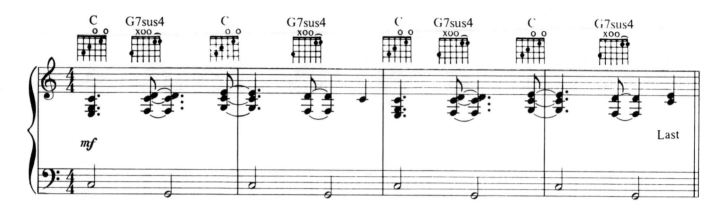

Moderately fast

mf

Last

night we brought_ the chil - dren by_ to vis - it their_ grand - pa._ And it's
day I took_ my wife_ for a walk down that old _ dirt road_ where my

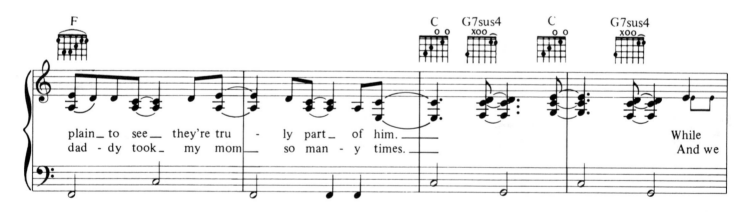

plain_ to see_ they're tru - ly part_ of him. _ While
dad - dy took_ my mom_ so man - y times. _ And we

we were there_ their grand - ma took_ out some old pho - to - graphs. _ Man,
found the time_ to men - tion things_ we nev - er had be - fore, _ and we

my fa - ther _ in me.

And to- _

And now

look-in' back,_ I can_ re-call_ the times_ we _ dis-a-greed._

And

I could not_ take hold _ of his_ old - fash-ioned ways._

And the

more I tried___ to prove___ him wrong___ the more___ I proved___ him right.___ Now I

know why he ___ still stood ___ by me ___ when I went through___ that stage.___ I'm see-in' my

*D.S. al Coda*

Coda

And I'm hap - py to see___ my fa -

ther ___ in me.___

*rit.*

127

# SHE CAME FROM FORT WORTH

## As recorded by KATHY MATTEA

Words and Music by
Pat Alger and Fred Koller

one - way __ tick - et on the next __ bus to Bould - er and it

won't __ take long to say good - bye. __ 1. She was

work - ing at a di - ner __ just a week a - go __ when a man __

2. *See additional lyrics*

__ from Col - o - ra - do __ smiled __ and said, "Hel - lo." And he turned __

her head with sto - ries 'bout a cab - in in the trees where the wind

can sing you love songs be - neath snow - capped moun - tain peaks.

Now she's packed her fad - ed blue jeans and her

fa - v'rite cow - boy boots, left her a - pron at the di - ner for some-

**Additional Lyrics**

2. And somewhere in the long dark night snow began to fall.
Oh, the world outside was sparkling white when she heard the driver call,
"Everyone off now for Boulder and have a real nice day."
He was waiting on the platform and he raised his hand away.
And she offered no resistance as he took her to his cabin,
And that diner in the distance seemed just like it never happened. *(To Chorus)*

# SOWIN' LOVE

As recorded by PAUL OVERSTREET

Words and Music by
Paul Overstreet and Don Schlitz

Lyrics:
How I used to love to walk be-hind my dad
How I used to love to sit and watch my ma-
dy ma as he plowed our gar-
ma work-in' with her nee-

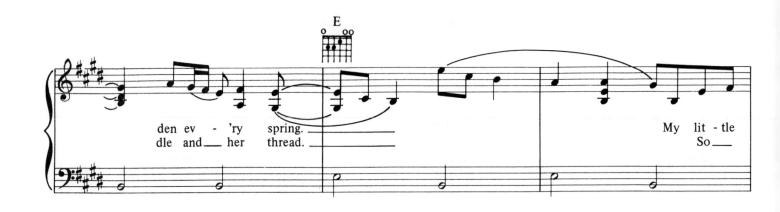

den ev - 'ry spring._____  My lit - tle
dle and__ her thread._____  So__

bare feet in the dirt___ would make__ me__ hap - py,  as we
pa - tient - ly she'd lis - ten to__ our__ prob - lems,  and

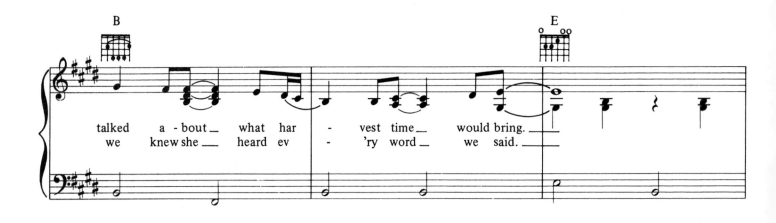

talked a - bout__ what har - vest time__ would bring.__
we knew she__ heard ev - 'ry word__ we said.__

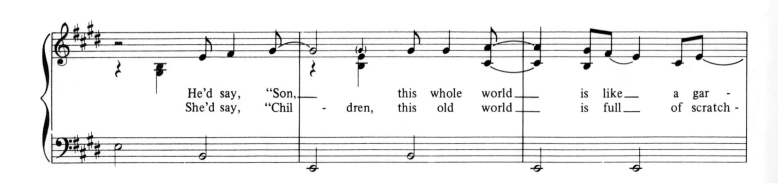

He'd say, "Son,__ this whole world__ is like__ a gar -
She'd say, "Chil - dren, this old world__ is full__ of scratch -

den,
es,
and
and
what you sow___ you're sure -
in your life___ you're bound___

ly gon - na reap.___
to have___ a few.___
Where
I

bit - ter seeds___ are plant - ed, hearts___ will hard - en,
guess that's why___ the good ___ Lord gave___ us patch - es,

but a car - ing hand___ will make___ the har - vest sweet."
so we could start ___ each day ___ out feel - ing new."

And he was sow - in'}
And she was sow - in'} love

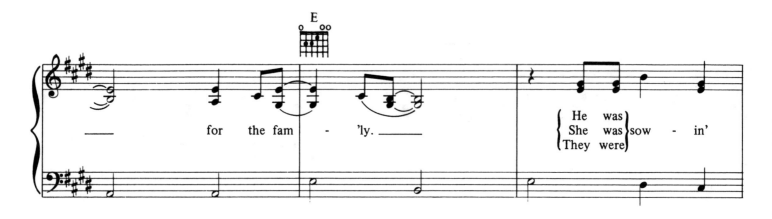

for the fam - 'ly. _____

{He was}
{She was} sow - in'
{They were}

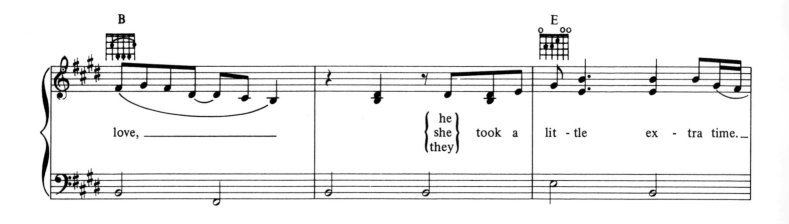

love, _____

{he}
{she} took a lit - tle ex - tra time. _
{they}

_____ Look - ing for - ward to _____ a boun - ti - ful har-

# TAKE ME HOME, COUNTRY ROADS

As recorded by JOHN DENVER

Words and Music by
John Denver, Bill Danoff
and Taffy Nivert

139

# STILL WITHIN THE SOUND OF MY VOICE

As recorded by GLEN CAMPBELL

Words and Music by
Jimmy Webb

# THIS LITTLE TOWN

## As recorded by DAVE MALLETT

Words and Music by
Dave Mallett

1. This lit-tle town__ is much the same as oth-ers I have known.__
2.3.4. *See additional lyrics*

Noth-in' much to do a-round here 'cept work __ and then go home.

*Recorded a half step lower.

Nev-er knew what his love___ was worth___ so he kept it on___ the shelf.___

Spend your mon-ey, spend your___ time,

*p* teach your chil - dren to be kind,___ they'll all come home at

Christ-mas time, and catch up on___ the news.___

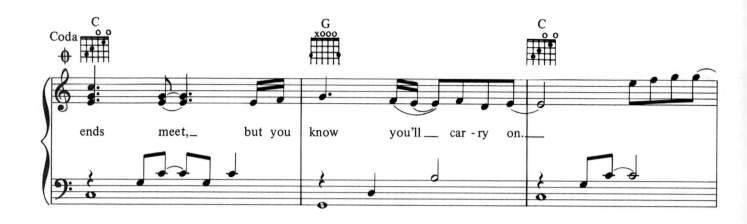

ends    meet,___    but you | know    you'll___ car - ry    on.___

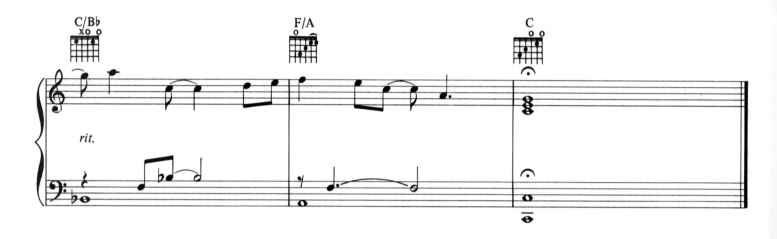

rit.

*Additional Lyrics*

2. Susan keeps the counter clean, Donald pumps the gas.
   Walter lives in yesterday 'cause today goes by too fast.
   TV nights and family fights, a young girl cryin' in the night
   'Cause she's lost the one that she thought was so right, a couple days ago. *(To Bridge)*

3. This little town is a quiet town; I've lived here for a while.
   Young girls dream of far away and learn to use their smile.
   Often marry much too young, give up when the party's done
   And dream of flight but never ever seem to run away.

4. *Repeat 1st Verse*

# WHEN I COULD COME HOME TO YOU

## As recorded by STEVE WARINER

Words and Music by
Steve Wariner and Roger Murrah

on the ra-di-o;___
I still wear,___

I love to hear___ it,      'cause
my heart's still wait-ing; it-'ll

you loved it so.___
al-ways be here.___

It re-minds me of___ the things___ we used to do,___
Do you ev-er think___ a-bout___ those days      too,___

when I could come home___ to you.___
when I could come home___ to you?___

Guess I'm___ just fool-ing my-self.___

I've al-ways___ been a   fool___ for you.___

# UNANSWERED PRAYERS

## As recorded by GARTH BROOKS

Words and Music by
Pat Alger, Garth Brooks
and Larry Bastian

mean he don't care. _____ Some of God's great-est gifts ____

are un - an - swered pray - ers. ____

*D.S. al Coda*

3. She

Coda

Lord knows ____ what he's do - in' af - ter ____ all. _____

And as she walked _ a - way _____ I

*Additional Lyrics*

2. She was the one that I wanted for all times,
   And each night I'd spend prayin' that God would make her mine.
   And if you'd only grant me this wish I wished back then,
   I'd never ask for anything again. *(To Chorus)*

3. She wasn't quite the angel
   That I remembered in my dreams,
   And I could tell the time changed me,
   In her eyes too it seemed.
   We tried to talk about the old days.
   Wasn't much we could recall.
   I guess the Lord knows what he's doin' after all. *etc.*

# WHEN YOU SAY NOTHING AT ALL

As recorded by KEITH WHITLEY

Words and Music by
Paul Overstreet and Don Schlitz

It's a-maz-ing how_ you can speak right_ to my heart.
All day long_ I can_ hear peo-ple talk-ing out loud,

With-out say-ing a word_ you can light up the dark.
but when you_ hold me near_ you drown out the crowd._

Try as I may_ I could nev-
Old Mis-ter Web-ster could nev-

er ex - plain___ what I hear___ when you don't ___ say a thing.
er de - fine___ what's be - ing said ___ be-tween your ___ heart and mine. ___

The

smile on your face ___ lets me know ___ that you need ___ me. There's a truth in your eyes ___ say - ing you'll ___

___ nev - er leave ___ me. A touch of your hand ___ says you'll catch ___ me if ev - er I fall. ___

*To Coda*

Now you say it best ___

# WHERE DID I GO WRONG

As recorded by STEVE WARINER

Words and Music by
Steve Wariner

# WICHITA LINEMAN

As recorded by GLEN CAMPBELL

Words and Music by
Jimmy Webb

Lyrics:

I am a line-man for the coun-ty, __ And I drive the main road

Search-in' in the sun for an - oth-er __ o - ver load. __
nev - er __ be __ the same. __

I hear you sing-in' in the wi - res
And I need you more than want you,

I can hear you thru the whine, __
And I want you for all time,

And the Wi - chi - ta Line - man is still on the line.
And the Wi - chi - ta Line - man is still on the line.

*To Coda*

I know I need a small va - ca - tion,

But it don't look like rain, And if it snows, that stretch down south will

*D.S. al ⊕ Coda*

⊕ *Coda*

# WRONG

## As recorded by WAYLON JENNINGS

Words and Music by
Andre Pessis and Steve Seskin

It was a pic - ture per - fect wed - ding,
I was all but dev - as - tat - ed

we had the whole world at our feet.
when she told me we were through.

Ev - 'ry one___ thought we were head - ing
In a while___ the heart - ache fad - ed,

down a lov - er's ea - sy street.
and I found some - bod - y new.

We'd have a house___ out in the coun - try,___
I swore that this___ time would be dif - f'rent;___

a pick - et fence, the whole nine___ yards.
I had it all fig - ured out.

They said our love would last for - ev - er,___
I would - n't make the same mis - takes;___

it was writ - ten in the stars.
I knew what love was all a - bout.

Wrong, I should have known it all a - long.

When the fu - ture looks too

bright, can't be an - y - thing but right.

*To Coda*

Wrong.

168

# ALPHABETICAL INDEX

4    Ace In The Hole

8    All The Fun

12    Annie's Song

16    Any Way The Wind Blows

20    Battle Hymn Of Love, The

24    Bayou Boys

30    Dance, The

34    Dear Me

27    Deeper Than The Holler

37    Diggin' Up Bones

40    Drive South

45    Flower That Shattered The Stone, The

52    Fly Away

49    Fly On The Wall

56    Folsom Prison Blues

58    Forever & Ever, Amen

62    Full Moon Full Of Love

68    Goin' Gone

72    Highwayman, The

65    Honky Tonk Moon

75    Houston Solution

78    I Fell In Love

82    I Won't Take Less Than Your Love

88    Lady

92    Love Chooses You

104    Love Or Something Like It

100    My Arms Stay Open All Night

112    Night's Too Long, The

97    On The Other Hand

109    Out Of Your Shoes

120    Postcard From Paris

117    Reckless Heart

124    Seein' My Father In Me

128    She Came From Fort Worth

133    Sowin' Love

141    Still Within The Sound Of My Voice

138    Take Me Home, Country Roads

146    This Little Town

154    Unanswered Prayers

151    When I Could Come Home To You

159    When You Say Nothing At All

162    Where Did I Go Wrong

164    Wichita Lineman

166    Wrong

The New York Times

# Country Music's Greatest Songs

ARRANGED AND EDITED BY
MILTON OKUN

NINETY-THREE SONGS FOR

VOICE

PIANO

GUITAR